T0208486

# TEN

# TEN

## LEVERAGING MARKETPLACE INFLUENCE

# MICHAEL D. KWAME

# TEN
## LEVERAGING MARKETPLACE INFLUENCE

Scripture quotations marked NLT are taken from the Holy Bible, New Living Translation, Copyright © 1996, 2004, 2007. Used by permission of Tyndale House Publishers, Inc. Carol Stream, Illinois 60188. All rights reserved. Website Scripture quotations marked NASB are taken from the New American Standard Bible®, Copyright © 1960, 1962, 1963, 1968, 1971, 1972, 1973, 1975, 1977, 1995 by The Lockman Foundation. Used by permission.

iUniverse books may be ordered through booksellers or by contacting:

iUniverse
1663 Liberty Drive
Bloomington, IN 47403
www.iuniverse.com
1-800-Authors (1-800-288-4677)

Because of the dynamic nature of the internet, any web addresses or links contained in this book may have changed since publication and may no longer be valid. The views expressed in this work are solely those of the author and do not necessarily reflect the views of the publisher, and the publisher hereby disclaims any responsibility for them.

Any people depicted in stock imagery provided by Getty Images are models, and such images are being used for illustrative purposes only.
Certain stock imagery © Getty Images.

ISBN: 978-1-6632-0013-6 (sc)
ISBN: 978-1-6632-0014-3 (e)

Library of Congress Control Number: 2020907931

Print information available on the last page.

iUniverse rev. date:  06/09/2020

# CONTENTS

# VIDEO RESOURCES

Marketplace Leadership
Networking
Winning HR
Entrepreneurship
Women in the Marketplace

# INTRODUCTION

I once fell into a trancelike state during an afternoon of devotion and prayer. While I may have been asleep, the suspension between consciousness and unconsciousness was not fully lucid. From a bird's-eye view, in this vision or dream of mine, I saw workers digging into the ground. The work was so dirty I could not identify their faces. Wearing what looked like overalls and helmets, they dug hard into the ground with their shovels. The atmosphere was saturated with a heavy brown haze, and I could hear the sound of raining sand. Yes, sand! I floated over these workers, watching from an aerial perspective their hard yet seemingly fruitless labor. They were tired, discouraged, and faint of heart, and I could feel their hearts yearning for true rain.

I have been working in human resources for more than five years, specializing in talent acquisition, training and development, and employee relations in the government contracting sector, and I believe my vision reveals the economic hardship of many professionals, families, businesses, organizations, cities, and nations. People work hard, but they still find emptiness and do not reap all the fruits of their labors.

You might find yourself in a tight market that does not seem to be opening to your business or professional skill set. Perhaps you are trying to survive in an economy that is limited in opportunities and yields little to no reward for the sweat of your brow. You feel as if you have been *digging* and have yet to get your first break. No business contracts. No promotions. No company has picked you up for hire.

I believe your economy is going to change for the better. I believe your days of planting and yielding no crops are coming to an end. A day is coming when economic recalcitrance will no longer be your portion. May financial drought over your career, family, business, city, and nation be broken. It is time to understand the power of *ten*.

## 10

The number ten in Hebrew has prophetic significance. The tenth letter of the Hebrew alphabet is *yod*. In modern Hebrew, you may see *yod* appear in the following forms:

*Yod* means "arm" or "hand." The arm or hand of God represents His power and intervention. It marks completion or order. God is looking to demonstrate His arm or hand through you in your place of work or business to set order and continuity in a way that reflects the culture and systematic process of the Kingdom.

The presence of God should be felt through you in the marketplace.

This book will help you do that. It uses the story of Daniel, who worked for the king of Babylon and was considered ten times wiser than other men, to relate biblical principles to the workplace today. Being *ten times better* in the marketplace isn't something that can be tracked numerically; it is achieved by possessing an excellent spirit in a way that makes you stand out.

Each chapter talks about one principle and relates it to Daniel's story so that you can use his example to develop your character in your workplace. In addition, this book contains links to videos to expand on the concepts.

May the rain you've been praying for come!

# CHAPTER 1

# The Competitive Edge

> The king talked with them, and out of them all not one was found like Daniel, Hananiah, Mishael and Azariah; so they entered the king's personal service. As for every matter of wisdom and understanding about which the king consulted them, he found them *ten times better* than all the magicians and conjurers who were in all his realm.
>
> —Daniel 1:19–20 (NASB; emphasis added)

The pressure of competition is always present. As an employee, you may ask what degree of value you bring to your employer compared to your colleagues that makes you worth keeping or promoting. Considering your spiritual side, as Daniel did, can help you navigate these competitive waters.

## Competition in Perspective

First, we should understand what healthy competition is and what it is not. Healthy competition is the drive to be the best version of *yourself.* It's the push to live out the potential endowed to you by the Creator. Yes, being the best version of *you* glorifies God. While others may emulate or imitate, there is no competition when it comes to being you! This is why you must focus on maximizing your potential to the fullest. You reign as champion in this space. No one can defeat you but *you*! This is an above-and-beyond mindset fueled by the conviction and desire to please God. The drive to stand out should not be misconstrued with people pleasing. People pleasing is a form of idol worship and will set you on the path to burnout and identity loss.

The scripture is clear:

> Slaves, in all things obey those who are your masters on earth, not with external service, as those who merely please men, but with sincerity of heart, fearing the Lord. Whatever you do, do your work heartily, as for the Lord rather than for men, knowing that from the Lord you will receive the reward of the inheritance. It is the Lord Christ whom you serve. (Colossians 3:22–24 NASB)

In whatever we put our hands to, Christ must be seen at the end of it. The driving force of excellence should stem from the desire to please Him, the epitome of excellence. This drive will shepherd you into becoming the best version of you.

The reason Daniel and his friends achieved excellence was they never compromised in Babylon, because of their passion to please God over the king. Not even the threat of a gruesome death could bring them to compromise, because they had the godly attributes of integrity and dedication to God. This faith in God influenced all aspects of their characters. Like Daniel, we also can submit ourselves to God and allow that posture to affect who we are and what we do.

Let's look at Daniel's story to learn more.

## Who, Me?

Daniel was in his teens to early twenties when he was taken into captivity by the Babylonian government. The king of Babylon, Nebuchadnezzar, had job openings in his cabinet for advisers. Those selected would undergo a three-year apprentice program. Nebuchadnezzar provided his chief of staff, Ashpenaz, with a brief job description for the ideal candidate that I imagine looked something like this:

| POSITION: ADVISER | DEPARTMENT: COURT OF ADVISERS |
|---|---|
| DIRECT SUPERVISOR: CHIEF OF OFFICIALS | GOVERNMENT: GREAT BABYLON |

**Purpose:** To act as an adviser to the great king in implementing political strategy.
**Qualifications:**
- healthy and handsome in appearance
- competent in various branches of learning

Indeed, the scripture says: "Select only strong, healthy, and good-looking young men … Make sure they are well versed in every branch of learning, are gifted with knowledge and good judgement, and are suited to serve in the royal palace" (Daniel 1:4 NLT).

Like most hiring managers today, the king wanted the best. Daniel was hired into the program for his healthy and handsome appearance and strong competence. But he had more than just good looks and intelligence. He had faith. The king noticed Daniel because he was different from the other men seeking the esteemed position. His spirit of integrity stood out from the rest. The basis of this was Daniel's faith in God, a faith that in turn inspired Daniel to grow and change according to the circumstances in which he found himself.

## The Power of Presence

At the age of seventeen, I recall attending a job fair to seek employment with a top retail grocery chain in South Texas. Determined to stand out from the competition, I put on my best French cuff shirt, tie, and slacks. I carried a folder, too, thinking it made me look serious. I felt how I looked—confident! I knew I stood out from the crowd of job seekers. I waited patiently for an interview, and my name was finally called. When I walked into the interview room, the interviewer looked at me from head to toe, examining my clothes. I was glad I had chosen to dress for success.

He whispered, "You have already won half the battle."

Yes, employers factor in appearance when making hiring decisions. Looking your professional best is critical.

Presence is what you wear and how you wear it coupled with what you believe about yourself (confidence). Human beings are visual and are moved by the external. Staying well-groomed and taking care of your body are factors in commanding presence. Interviewers make assumptions at first sight. Prospective clients also take note of your presence when you make a proposal pitch. Your presence has a handshake that greets others before you do. How you feel about yourself—and how you feel about your potential employer—is reflected in how you dress and carry yourself. Perfect and watch your body language!

## The Value of Competence

What you know and understand is a sign to an employer or prospective client of the value you bring to the table. How well versed are you in your industry or line of business? How much reading and research have you done? What is your problem-solving process? Do you have a college degree or specialized certification? How much experience do you have? These things are easy to express. You can even put them on a résumé. But when you talk to someone and demonstrate that you know what matters to him or her, that person can visualize you fitting in, and he or she will want to help you.

Take time to find information about the company and position for which you are applying. Research the company and talk to employees who work there if you can. This approach itself is a form of competence, and competence gives you leverage to solve problems. You are only as valuable as the problems you can solve in the marketplace.

So how do you get this competence? Competence has two components: experience and education. Experience is what you have done so far in your career and what you have learned that makes you adaptable and an asset to your employer. Education (both formal and informal) is also key to cultivating competence. Always be a seeker of knowledge and understanding, not only in school but also in your life experiences.

## Putting Competence and Presence Together

Daniel's competence affected his presence and served as the starting point for what made him and his friends *ten times better* than all others. You, too, can apply this in your life by thinking about how others see your choices in clothing, grooming, and attitude, as well as by working on your internal relationship with the Spirit. Pay attention to those around you and be self-aware.

# CHAPTER 2

# Adaptability

> In the third year of the reign of Jehoiakim king of Judah, Nebuchadnezzar king of Babylon came to Jerusalem and besieged it. The Lord gave Jehoiakim king of Judah into his hand.
>
> —Daniel 1:1–2 (NASB)

Very few people do the same thing every day. Change is inevitable, even if it happens slowly. Sometimes the change is external. For example, a company is bought out or the people we work with and work for change. Other times, the changes are internal because we grow and need new challenges. Most careers, and growth, require us to adapt.

For Babylon, exile was a political tactic of intimidation. This power play was strategic in that it showed economically weaker countries who was in charge and manipulated rulers into sending tax money to the empire or risk losing top-tier citizens. Forced exile was big business. These kinds of political takeovers created changes in leadership, culture, belief systems, socioeconomics, laws, and so on.

Daniel lived through two empires (Babylon and Persia) and advised more than one king. Imagine the culture shock he experienced. Interestingly enough, Babylon's forced exile on Judah was a fulfillment of prophecy, and Daniel had to adapt to express the power of the Kingdom in a pagan society.

## Breathe, Stretch, Shake, and Let Go

Have you ever worked for an organization experiencing change in executive leadership, struggled to do business in a new market, or worked for a company newly acquired by another? In your current job function or business, perhaps things keep changing and you are fighting to stay afloat in perilous waters. Maybe your place of employment is experiencing high turnover and you find yourself feeling the burden of it. Or perhaps your workplace is transitioning to a new applicant tracking system (ATS) and you are responsible for spearheading the change. It isn't easy! Breakthroughs in technological advances and paradigm shifts in thinking continue to rise. The pressure to "breathe, stretch, shake, and let go" of the old to embrace the new is constant.

Today's marketplace demands adaptability. Adapting simply means (a) to make fit or suitable by changing or adjusting or (b) to adjust oneself to new or changed circumstances.

Adapting implies flexibility. Irrespective of your personality type, to stay ahead in today's culture, you cannot afford to be recalcitrant to change! Companies are losing because of lack of flexibility, and job applicants are missing opportunities because they are not privy to shifts in the job market. Knowing how to increase your adaptability will give you an edge.

## What Employers Want

A recent LinkedIn study showed that 69 percent of hiring managers view adaptability as the most important soft skill they screen for because of economic changes and business needs.[1] I predict this number will continue to rise. Entrepreneurs can also take note of this, as consumers want convenience and seek to know how your product or service can meet their changing needs compared to your competitors.

Here are a few common interview questions[2] employers ask to test a candidate's adaptability skill set:

1.  Tell me about a time you were asked to do something you had never done before. How did you react? What did you learn?
2.  Describe a situation in which you embraced a new system, process, technology, or idea at work that was a major departure from the *old way* of doing things.

---

[1] Lydia Abbot, Maria Ignatova, and Allison Schnidman, *30 Behavioral Interview Questions to Identify High-Potential Candidates* (LinkedIn Talent Solutions, 2017).
[2] Abbot, Ignatova, and Schnidman, *30 Behavioral Interview Questions*.

3. Recall a time when you were assigned a task outside your job description. How did you handle the situation? What was the outcome?
4. Tell me about the biggest change you have had to deal with. How did you adapt to that change?
5. Tell me about a time you had to adjust to a colleague's working style in order to complete a project or achieve your objectives.

How would you answer these questions in an interview? Why does change fluster you, if at all? Adaptability enhances your marketability and requires a solution-oriented mind-set. Professionally speaking, what recent problems have you solved as a result of your adaptability? Like Daniel, can you implement solutions to complex matters of kings (upper management)? If so, promotion is inevitable! Allow God to use your changing environment to stretch your capacity.

## Finding Your Adaptability

It can be hard to evaluate where we need to grow to become adaptable. But as you look at yourself, consider the things you are not willing to do and then ask if they are things you can change or learn. If there is something you are resisting, look at it as an area for potential growth. You could also go to conventions, join associations, subscribe to magazines, find people in your industry or on social media, and take classes or go back to school. The more you learn, the more knowledge you can apply to the circumstances and problems around you and the more you will be able to adapt to changing needs.

# CHAPTER 3

# Babylon's Table

> But Daniel made up his mind that he would not defile himself with the king's choice food or with the wine which he drank ... But Daniel said to the overseer whom the commander of the officials had appointed ... Please test your servants for *ten days*, and let us be given some vegetables to eat and water to drink.
>
> —Daniel 1:8, 11–12 (NASB; emphasis added)

When people climb the professional ranks, sometimes their appetites (desires) change. The use and desire for power become corrupt, and greed settles in, resulting in white-collar crimes, manipulation, dishonesty, control, acts of sexual immorality, pride, arrogance, and so on. If your name (sense of identity) and appetites (desires) have changed for the worse, you have had fellowship at Babylon's table.

## You Are Not Your Title

Daniel, highly esteemed, did not allow his given Babylonian name and professional title to define him. Likewise, your job title is simply your job function in how you are to serve others. It is not something to brag about; your title is responsibility! Neither should it become so important that you lose sight of things in life outside your job as you climb the professional ladder.

Many professionals lose themselves and handicap their futures by chasing and living for their careers. You may climb all the way up the ladder only to look down and see that

- your marriage is on the verge of divorce;
- your children resent you for not being present enough;
- you always have an excuse for not finishing your degree;
- your health is declining;
- you never started your business venture;
- you passed up opportunities for marriage and family building; or
- your local church gets little to none of your commitment.

It was common during Daniel's time for men serving the royal court to be castrated to make them reliable servants or slaves to the king. Today, many ambitious professionals have been spiritually castrated and are impotent in their ability to produce in all other areas of their lives except for their kings (employers). Even ambitious clergy get caught in the trap of trying to build ministry empires at the expense of their own families. Yes, you can be in ministry and still dine at Babylon's table! Executive director, chief, president, operations manager, doctor, pastor, and so on—get over yourself! If stripped of your title and job, who are you? Find your balance and cultivate humility. Invest in others, yourself, your family, and your community because they are more important than vain pursuits.

## Strange Food

When Daniel entered the king's court, Nebuchadnezzar developed an implementation strategy to strip him of his Jewish identity. He changed Daniel's *name* (to Belshazzar) and his *diet* to socialize him in Babylonian culture. Daniel refused to partake at Babylon's table because the first portion of the food was offered to idols. Moreover, the wine was poured out on pagan altars.

Refusing to defile himself with the king's food, Daniel kept his appetite pure in terms of what he knew was pleasing to God. He experienced promotion and received honor even when he remained faithful to his convictions, and this honor was greater than Daniel could have imagined at first.

## What a Title Should Be

Compromising values for selfish gain is for the weak, but the risk of courage is reserved for system shakers. In the business world, this might mean a person focuses less on amassing a title for him- or herself and more on developing those around him or her to achieve success. This is what it means to view your title as how you may serve others, while also keeping sight of your duties to your family and community. It also means conducting oneself with integrity, being someone others can look to for sound leadership, and making the corporate environment a better place.

# CHAPTER 4

# The Lion's Mouth

> Then the king gave orders, and Daniel was brought in and cast into the lions den ... A stone was brought and laid over the mouth of the den.
>
> —Daniel 6:16–17 (NASB)

There may come a time in your professional life when your back is forced against a wall, not because you have done anything wrong but because of your integrity and excellent spirit. People will not always appreciate your optimistic attitude, competence, and willingness to collaborate. In the minds of the insecure, your success is a threat to their upward mobility. They fear you will take their place or rank higher than them. At these points, you may be asked to compromise your ethics and even your morality. Daniel also had to make these considerations. Let's look at what he chose.

MICHAEL D. KWAME

## Power Play

King Darius had the vision to appoint Daniel as one of three commissioners over 120 satraps (provincial governors or local rulers) to be in charge of the whole kingdom.

> It seemed good to Darius to appoint 120 satraps over the kingdom, that they would be in charge of the whole kingdom, and over them three commissioners (of whom Daniel was one), that these satraps might be accountable to them, and that the king might not suffer loss. Then this Daniel began distinguishing himself among the commissioners and satraps because he possessed an extraordinary spirit, and the king planned to appoint him over the entire kingdom. (Daniel 6:1–3 NASB)

Daniel had an excellent spirit in his approach to his work. The king recognized his surpassing skill set and wanted to appoint him over the entire kingdom! His excellent spirit had distinguished him from everyone else. This caused jealousy among his colleagues.

> Then the commissioners and satraps began trying to find a ground of accusation against Daniel in regard to government affairs; but they could find no ground of accusation or evidence of corruption, inasmuch as he was faithful, and no negligence or corruption was to be found in him. Then these men

> said, "We will not find any ground of
> accusation against this Daniel unless we
> find it against him with regard to the law
> of his God." (Daniel 6:4–5 NASB)

Sound familiar? Daniels's colleagues set the power play in motion to position him for demise. Fortunately, Daniel walked in such strong integrity that they could find no trace of dirt on him. As a result, they formulated a political strategy to use his faith against him.

## Politics in the Workplace

Politics have been part of the workplace since the very beginning. Daniel was no exception. The executive leadership of the Persian empire advised the king to put a thirty-day law into place. This law prohibited anyone from praying to a figure other than King Darius himself. According to Persian law, once an injunction was signed, it could not be revoked. The king, deceived into believing that Daniel had a part in the matter, signed the law into action. Any violator of the law would be thrown into a den of lions. Aware that Daniel was well rooted and disciplined in his faith, his colleagues knew he would not submit to such a law.

When Daniel learned of the newly signed injunction, he continued to pray to his God three times a day and refused to compromise. Daniel was caught praying and brought to King Darius, who was distressed and did not realize that Daniel was the victim of a political scheme. The king could not veto the law to save him, and Daniel was thrown into a den of lions, but God delivered him.

> A stone was brought and laid over the mouth of the den; and the king sealed it with his own signet ring and with the signet rings of his nobles, so that nothing would be changed in regard to Daniel … Then the king arose at dawn, at the break of day, and went in haste to the lions' den … Then Daniel spoke to the king … My God sent His angel and shut the lions' mouths and they have not harmed me. (Daniel 6:17, 19, 21–22 NASB)

God intervened! In a den of hungry lions, the King of kings sent an angel to shut their mouths. The lion's mouth manifests when a system comes against you unjustly to destroy your name and credibility. The system could not devour Daniel. The same God who vindicated him is the same God who can vindicate you from any false accusation or political game to put your life, career, name, or business in jeopardy! For Daniel's sake, justice was administered.

> The king then gave orders, and they brought those men who had maliciously accused Daniel, and they cast them, their children and their wives into the lions' den; and they had not reached the bottom of the den before the lions overpowered them and crushed all their bones. (Daniel 6:24 NASB)

When we are vindicated, it is not for us to retaliate. Divine justice is a law and has a way of coming back around full circle.

I have witnessed people of power in the workplace conspiring against others unjustly to get them fired. Once time came around for layoffs, they were let go, while their victims remained with the company. Even if you lose a job unjustly, is not your future secure in God? Indeed it is, and justice will come in its time! Follow Daniel's example and behave in accordance with what God has taught you. No matter the political pressure you are facing right now in your business or job, God can deliver you from the lion's mouth!

# CHAPTER 5

# Leadership

> Then this Daniel began distinguishing himself among the commissioners and satraps because he possessed an extraordinary spirit, and the king planned to appoint him over the entire kingdom.
>
> —Daniel 6:3 (NASB)

Every sphere of influence in society is crying out for effective leadership, and in some ways, this is very clear in the corporate world. While there are many definitions of leadership, it can simply be defined as "influence" or, according to Wesley Shotwell, "an ability to move people from one reality to another."[3] Organizations are looking for movement, and it takes effective leadership to shift paradigms and see vision fulfilled. One of the key elements of leveraging advantage in the marketplace is leadership

---

[3] Wesley Shotwell, *The Power of Being a Servant* (Keller: Austin Brothers Publishing, 2011).

capacity, and companies must identify who the leaders in their organizations can be. Will it be you?

It can be you. But to influence another person, you must first have his or her trust.

## The Leadership Formula

For certain, two qualities that made Daniel an ideal leader of his time were character and competence, as noted in an earlier chapter. These same characteristics are needed in the workforce to win the trust of colleagues and upper management. If you operate your own business, customers are looking for you to have integrity and thorough knowledge in your service or product. In his book *The Power of Being a Servant*, Wesley Shotwell lays out the Trust Formula regarding leadership in a mathematic equation:

Trustworthiness = [consistency (character + competence)]$^{\text{TIME}}$

To further define the formula, he states, "In other words, trustworthiness equals consistent character plus consistent competence factored by the length of time a person has experienced these qualities."[4]

Daniel exhibited this type of trustworthiness, and God, through the king, rewarded it. Daniel was part of this equation also because he continued growing his knowledge of the things that fell within the scope of his job, so he became a competent leader who leveraged trust.

---

[4] Shotwell, *The Power of Being a Servant*.

The same could be true of you. Cultivate your character and your competence. Study the Bible and continue studying for your job. Stay up to date on trends and ask about educational opportunities in your company so you can grow.

You aren't the only one interested in your leadership potential. Your company is looking at it also.

## Growth Potential

A LinkedIn survey suggests that when an employee leaves an organization, on average, it costs the company 1.5 times that employee's salary to replace them. Employers are aware that screening for leadership and growth potential can save their organization money. They want to know how you fit their succession strategy. Leadership and growth potential are how you position yourself for advancement.

Here are some questions to consider when employers are screening for leadership and growth potential. Think about and refine your answers as you read these questions.

## Leadership Screening Questions

1. Tell me about the last time something significant didn't go according to plan at work. What was your role? What was the outcome?
2. Describe a situation where you needed to persuade someone to see things your way. What steps did you take? What were the results?

3.  Give me an example of a time when you felt you led by example. What did you do and how did others react?
4.  Tell me about the toughest decision you had to make in the last six months.
5.  Have you ever had to "sell" an idea to your coworkers or group? How did you do it? What were the results?[5]

## Growth Potential Screening Questions

1.  Recall a time when your manager was unavailable when a problem arose. How did you handle the situation? With whom did you consult?
2.  Describe a time when you volunteered to expand your knowledge at work, as opposed to being directed to do so.
3.  What would motivate you to make a move from your current role?
4.  When was the last occasion you asked for direct feedback from a supervisor? Why?
5.  What's the biggest career goal you've ever achieved?[6]

Revisit these questions periodically. Your answers can reflect your growth as a leader and improve your growth potential, which can inspire trust and make you valuable to your company.

---

[5] Abbot, Ignatova, and Schnidman, *30 Behavioral Interview Questions*.

[6] Abbot, Ignatova, and Schnidman, *30 Behavioral Interview Questions*.

# TEN

## Beyond the Read
### *Marketplace Leadership*

Watch a video segment between Michael Kwame
and Richard Namme on marketplace leadership.
thebookten.com
Access Code: DanielTEN

# CHAPTER 6

# **Networking**

> Then the king promoted Daniel … and he made him ruler over the whole province of Babylon and chief prefect over all the wise men of Babylon. And Daniel *made request* of the king, and he appointed Shadrach, Meshack and Abed-nego over the administration of the province of Babylon, while Daniel was at the king's court.
>
> —Daniel 2:48–49 (NASB; emphasis added)

It's not what you know but who you know, right? A network is a connection or link. Networking is social currency cultivated through relationships, but it's most effective if those relationships are genuine and reciprocal. Just about every job I have had has resulted from a network or networking. Have you ever witnessed someone get hired into a specific company, organization, or position and wondered how he or she got in? Who did that person know? What did he or she do? It's often a result of networking. The people you know have keys. People are willing to open doors to you when your networking is genuine and potential is recognized.

In the scripture above (Daniel 2:48–49), when Daniel was promoted to high rank, he "made request" of the king regarding his friends. As a result, they were promoted to preside over the administration of the province of Babylon. To *make request* in the aforementioned scripture means "to seek (for favor)," "to ask," "to desire," or "to make petition." The root meaning is "to swell, to boil up, to gush over." Upon promotion, when Daniel went before the king about his friends, not only did he use his influence to make mention of them but I believe he talked them up and spoke highly of them (swelled, boiled up, gushed over) for this new role in the kingdom. This happens in the business world when someone you know talks highly about you to a hiring manager. This is what happens behind the scenes in professional workspaces. A person refers someone to a decision maker and *swells* or *boils* him or her up in recommendation. For Daniel, this was not the case of a hookup per se. His network of friends actually possessed the intellectual capacity and character for the job. Daniel did not lie. The genuine relationship Daniel's friends cultivated with him created a network and opened doors for them.

## Ships: What Networking Is

God is a God of relationships. Notice the fourth syllable in the word *relationship* is the word *ship*. A ship is a cargo vessel, a means for transporting people or goods from one place to another. People hold the capacity to move you from one place to the next, for better or for worse. In every network or connection you make, you must ask yourself: What is the destination of this *ship*? What motives are involved? What is the bigger picture? What does this person or organization have that I need? What does this person or organization expect from me? Where could this take me? What role am I to play in the movement of the *ship*?

No one is equipped to accomplish his or her vision by him- or herself. Networking and relationships are required.

I recall a time when I was at the boxing gym, working the mitts with my coach in the middle of the ring. I heard a man say, "It's time for me to head back to work." Following my conviction, I immediately paused my workout to ask him, "What do you do?" I stepped out of the ring, and he and I began to converse (network). It turned out, he was a pharmacy area manager for a prominent retail store, a company my wife (a pharmacy student at the time) had prayed about that week, unbeknownst to me. The gentleman gave me his card, and within a few months, my wife was hired on as a pharmacy intern! The process was effortless. When networking, you must obey the inner signals of the Spirit to reach out to someone and spark a conversation. I often wonder how my wife's professional path would have been altered had I disregarded the inner prompting to connect with a complete stranger. God uses the vehicle of human beings to express His favor.

Networking means many things:

- having a genuine conversation that isn't about selling something but instead about following the prompts of your spirit to connect

- intentional, long-term relationship building
- genuinely listening to another person
- further developing social and professional contacts related to your business or interests
- being helpful to others (e.g., sharing industry knowledge)

## What Networking Is Not

For clarity's sake, it is critical that I make clear what networking is not:

- a "hookup" (Referrals should be based on proven capacity, not lies.)
- people pleasing
- compromising moral values for acceptance
- using others for selfish ambition
- getting over on others to move up
- a means to immediate monetary gain

## Opportunities for Networking

There are many ways to network, depending on your objective and how close you are to opportunities. You can network virtually anywhere merely by talking to someone. Some ideas include the following:

- college (professors, peers)
- internships (building a network inside a company)
- associations

- LinkedIn
- business mixers
- job fairs
- jury duty
- airports
- mentorship
- seminars
- volunteering

## Bridge Building

Networking is not always about what you can get but about what you can give. Use your influence to change lives by creating and extending opportunities to others. When Daniel was promoted, he did not forget about his friends. He used his influence as a bridge for others. Sometimes people who move up professionally or financially assimilate and disregard those who labored with them prior to their good fortune. Remember when you were the vulnerable outsider looking for someone to pull you in? Do you recall how you finally got into that organization after your hundredth application? You did not always have that master's degree, did you? At the pinnacle of professional achievement, you are never *too busy* to build a bridge.

# TEN

## Beyond the Read
## *Networking*

Watch a video segment between Michael
Kwame and Tony Moore on networking.
thebookten.com
Access code: DanielTEN

# TEN

## Beyond the Read
### *Winning HR*

Watch a video segment between Michael Kwame and
Tony Moore on understanding human resources.
thebookten.com
Access code: DanielTEN

**CHAPTER 7**

# A Call to Integrity

> Then the commissioners and satraps began trying to find a ground of accusation against Daniel in regard to government affairs; but they could find no ground of accusation or evidence of corruption, inasmuch as he was faithful, and no negligence or corruption was to be found in him.
>
> —Daniel 6:4 (NASB)

## The Ethical Dimension

Integrity is the state of being whole or undivided. Uncovered or not, breaches in professionalism, from perpetual late returns from lunch breaks to executive white-collar crime, are manifestations of a divided or broken individual. While competence and determination can take you far, integrity is what sustains you. As it states in Daniel 6:4, no evidence of corruption was found in Daniel's professional function.

His integrity was so strong that his enemies had to find a way to use his faith against him.

We need professionals who refuse to be bought! No bonus, exotic trip, drug, sexual advance, promotion, stock option, money, notoriety, or other factor should shift your integrity paradigm. This is a call of accountability to all professionals in every industry to commit to doing what is right. Individuals, companies, organizations, governments, politicians, church leaders, entrepreneurs, and others are divided behind ambition and thirst for power. Even the person with the least esteemed job in a company is not excluded. This is a call for employers to do right by their employees and for employees to do right by their employers. Corruption concealed is destined to be revealed.

## Telecom Cowboy

In the 1990s, a company established in Clinton, Mississippi, in 1983 experienced tremendous growth. The telecommunications firm became second to AT&T and leveraged marketplace influence through a succession of takeovers. The company had even planned a $115 billion Sprint acquisition that was vetoed by US and European regulators. To artificially increase the company's net income, the company capitalized expenses and recorded costs as assets, which resulted in an inflated net income of more than $7.6 billion between the years of 1999 and 2002. Top executives were given retention bonuses of $10 million and allocations of millions of stock options.

The company's financial statement fraud led to a total damage of $11 billion. In an attempt to meet Wall

Street's expectations, the company falsified accounting records. In July 2002, the company declared bankruptcy. A former employee claimed in court that he was told to "hit the numbers." The CEO, along with other perpetrating employees, were fined and imprisoned. A man with seemingly unlimited power, Bernard Ebbers, the Telecom Cowboy, founder of WorldCom, had engineered one of the biggest scandals in American history.[7]

## Guard Your Brand

Having integrity makes you wise to the ways of the world. It is important to protect yourself from those who have no integrity. Your name, the way others perceive you, is your brand. In business, we all know how important it is to manage your brand. The same applies to yourself.

When I was facilitating a training class for a group of HR professionals, I put together a creative icebreaker. I held up symbols of well-known brands and asked participants to state the adjectives that came to mind. When I held up the famous Apple logo, the class described the brand as innovative, cutting edge, tech centric, out of the box, and quality. At the end of the presentation, I followed up with a rhetorical question to the group: "If your name was displayed in front of an audience of people you knew, how would your character and work ethic be described in your absence?" I then instructed them to write a letter to themselves describing what they wanted their personal and

---

[7] Leonard Brooks and Paul Dunn, *Business and Professional Ethics* (Boston: Cengage Learning, 2015).

professional brands to be. All the participants opted to have me mail their letters to them at a future unexpected time.

Your name is an enterprise shadowed by adjectives! You are the CEO of your personal brand, and the responsibility of quality professional development falls on you. Every decision you make affects your brand. Consider the following:

- How did you leave your last two to three employers? It has been said that it is a small world, and this is true. You never know who you will meet later, so you wouldn't want your brand to be that you are someone who left the company in a lurch by not giving notice or by bad-mouthing your boss.

- On average, how long do you stay with an employer? There is no hard-and-fast rule for this, but in general, it's not favorable to look like you change jobs every three months. Things take time to fully evaluate, so try to stay for at least a year.

- If your résumé were a story, what would it say about you? Is there a lot of ambiguity (e.g., consistent employment gaps, job-hopping)? Evaluate your résumé from another person's perspective. No one has the perfect résumé, but there are ways to present what you've done that emphasize the positive. Contact a professional if you feel you need help.

- Do you think things through and seek wise counsel before making decisions? Only you can evaluate how well this is occurring for you. If you find room for improvement, implement the necessary changes.

- How credible are your references? Your references should be as recent as possible. They should be people who worked with you, not your friends, and if possible, people who have relevant insight into the job you're seeking.

- Have you ever been fired? If the answer is yes, don't dodge the question or bad-mouth your former employer. Think about the lessons you've learned. How have you grown?
- Have you ever resigned in lieu of being fired?
- Does your résumé tell the truth about you?

Trust can be challenging to leverage, but how much more difficult is it to rebuild once it's been breached? Nothing builds credibility like a good name built on integrity.

# CHAPTER 8

# Revelation Knowledge

> The king answered Daniel and said, "Surely your God is a God of gods and a Lord of kings and a revealer of mysteries, since you have been able to reveal this mystery." Then the king promoted Daniel and gave him many great gifts, and he made him ruler over the whole province of Babylon and chief prefect over all wise men of Babylon.
>
> —Daniel 2:47–48 (NASB)

Word of knowledge is a supernatural download of facts and information from the mind of God about someone or something. This supernatural knowledge transcends natural knowledge and reveals what is hidden or concealed. Word of knowledge is a revelation gift God has made accessible to His children by His Spirit.

When faced with death, Daniel sought God in prayer regarding the king's dream and received downloaded information from heaven that told him what Nebuchadnezzar had dreamed and what his dream meant. This revelation gift is applicable to the marketplace, and when it manifests, the most powerful leaders in any organization, corporation, or government will bow. Nebuchadnezzar is a great example of this.

## When Kings Dream

Daniel had a special ability that made him most distinct: revelation knowledge. He was prophetically inclined to the future and had word of knowledge concerning mysteries that his own peers and the king could not decode. King Nebuchadnezzar had a dream about the future that he could not understand. He summoned his team of magicians, enchanters, sorcerers, and astrologers to tell him what he dreamed and provide the interpretation. If they could not fulfill the two-part request, the king would have them all put to death. Flustered by a seemingly impossible request, Nebuchadnezzar's cabinet of sorcerers was unable to fulfill it. Upon the decree of death, Daniel took on the challenge and prayed to God overnight, and the mystery was unveiled to him. Yes, God showed Daniel exactly what the king had dreamed and what it meant. This prophetic insight provided to Daniel gave Nebuchadnezzar insight on the future of his government and emerging kingdoms thereafter. This victory brought glory to God and a promotion for Daniel.

CEOs, politicians, business owners, and executives are concerned with the future state of what they are responsible for stewarding. They also want to understand the complexities and solutions to their everyday business problems. Kings (people of authority) are looking for people with in-depth insights into their challenges who can extract solutions. Promotion comes to those who can transcend complaining about problems and provide customized solutions to complex issues.

## Word of Knowledge

> Now concerning spiritual gifts, brethren, I do not want you to be unaware ... For to one is given the word of wisdom through the Spirit, and to another the *word of knowledge* according to the same Spirit.
>
> —1 Corinthians 12:1, 8 (NASB; emphasis added)

> Then king Nebuchadnezzar fell on his face and did homage to Daniel, and gave orders to present to him an offering and fragrant incense.
>
> —Daniel 2:46 (NASB)

King Nebuchadnezzar was in total awe that God had revealed such information to Daniel. He was so moved that he fell on his face and promoted him. By no means does this gift make any human all-knowing or equal to God. God created such revelatory insight to bring Him glory alone and to allow the vessel He is using to leverage influence for the advancement of His Kingdom. Honor and promotion are by-products of this gift.

Here is a true modern story and example of how this gift can work in the marketplace:

> I was playing a game on my phone when I saw a picture in my mind's eye. In my head, I could clearly see my friends named James and Susan. The mental image stayed, and pretty soon I realized it wasn't just a random memory coming up. God was trying to get my attention …
>
> That's when I received what I felt was a direct feed from the heart and mind of God for a different James and Susan. I immediately had knowledge about them. It's hard to explain, but it was like I was sharing so deeply in God's thoughts that they felt organic to my own. What was in His imagination and thoughts had merged with my own …
>
> The good friends we were meeting had brought another couple to tag along with us at dinner. I was glad to meet this beautiful couple but knew this wasn't just a nice social gathering when they told me their names: Jim (James) and Sue (Susan)! …
>
> "Are your kids' names Olivia and Samuel?" I asked.

They smiled and nodded, trying to figure out how I knew this …

"I feel like God is showing me that you have been through the hardest financial battle of your life but that He is with you and is going to help you … I then saw a yellow rain jacket, and it was being folded up and had a price tag on it. I saw it selling for a really high price and saw you guys walking into a huge manufacturing plant with plans for a new, way better rain jacket that had global distribution."

They sat in shock. Sue was crying lightly. "Does the rain jacket mean something to you?" I asked. They nodded and explained that they were part owners in a company called Rain Jacket. They were currently in a lawsuit with other owners, which had been ruining their lives. They had been praying about selling their share and starting something else. They were wonderful Christians who were praying about this situation, but they didn't know they could hear from God about it.[8]

---

[8] Shawn Bolz, *God's Secrets: A Life Filled with Words of Knowledge* (Studio City: ICreate Productions, 2017).

God wants to make Himself present through you in a revelatory way in your place of work, start-up, political office, and so on. The scripture says, "It is the glory of God to conceal a matter, but the glory of kings is to search out a matter" (Proverbs 25:2 NASB).

Leaders in every sphere of influence are searching for solutions to their complex problems. Who will seek Him for word of knowledge to crack the code and create breakthroughs in the affairs of humanity? I believe there are things that God has purposefully concealed for us to seek out. We find them by seeking God in prayer, being honest with ourselves in what we discover, cultivating our strengths, resolving our shortcomings, and adhering to His voice. Daniel sought out what God concealed and used this gift to advise his employer. I see a day in which the gift of word of knowledge is going to increase and influence the marketplace in a greater measure.

# CHAPTER 9

# The Technology of Prayer

> And he continued kneeling on his knees three times a day, praying and giving thanks before his God, as he had been doing previously.
>
> —Daniel 6:10 (NASB)

Stress is a big issue for almost anyone in the workplace today. And stress and anxiety can carry over into our home lives and impede our ability to grow with God. There are several weapons you can use in the battle against stress and anxiety, and prayer is one of them.

Prayer is the channel of communication between God and people. It's a method that brings the natural and spiritual worlds together. Prayer is the key that grants you access to a higher realm and activates the machinery of heaven. God is often painted as a cruel and unrelatable force far above the clouds, anxiously waiting to judge our mistakes. This psychological portrait is erroneous. While supernatural, He is still accessible. While omnipotent, He is still loving and gracious and desires to speak to us.

## War on Stress and Anxiety

It seems stress and anxiety are at an all-time high. You don't have to look far to see how it affects people; just look at the way they drive. According to everydayhealth.com, in 2018 stress was at an all-time high for twenty- to twenty-five-year-olds.[9]

I hear people talking about their battles with stress and anxiety more now than ever before. With technological advancements, everything around us moves faster and faster. We all feel the weight of expectations in our businesses, workplaces, schools, homes, ministries, and so on. Nothing is slowing down. In response to this changing environment, we suffer from panic attacks, depression, insomnia, distress, and health scares. No six-figure salary can buy you joy, peace, and balance. Distress and anxiety are affecting people of all socioeconomic statuses.

Richard A. Swenson, MD, defines the term *margin* as the space between our load and our limits, the gap between rest and exhaustion, the space between breathing freely and suffocating.[10] Are you suffocating emotionally from the weight of responsibility that you carry? Is your health at risk? Has your personality changed for the worse? Are you consistently missing significant moments with those who

---

[9]  Marie Connolly and Margot Slade, "The United States of Stress 2019," Everyday Health, last modified May 7, 2019, https://www.everydayhealth.com/wellness/united-states-of-stress.

[10]  Richard A. Swenson, *Margin* (Colorado Springs: NavPress, 2004).

matter most to you? Stress and anxiety can rob you of life if you allow it. You have the power to implement balance, or *margin*.

Swenson provides the following formula for leveraging margin (balance):

$$\text{Power} - \text{Load} = \text{Margin}$$

Power comes from energy, skills, time, training, emotional and physical strength, faith, finances, and social supports. Load is made up of work, problems, obligations and commitments, expectations (internal and external), debt, deadlines, and interpersonal conflicts. When the load surpasses our power, we enter into a negative margin status.[11] The negative margin status is distress, anxiety, overload, and imbalance.

## Daniel Understood Stress

The scriptures reveal what David understood about prayer and anxiety:

> Be anxious for nothing, but in everything by *prayer* and supplication with thanksgiving let your requests be made known to God. And the peace of God, which surpasses all comprehension, will guard your hearts and your minds in Christ Jesus. (Philippians 4:6–7 NASB; emphasis added)

---

[11] Swenson, *Margin*.

Prayer is a weapon against anxiety! Do you think Daniel felt any pressure or stress? He sure did. But Daniel picked up God's weapon against stress. He prayed three times a day and gave thanks to God consistently. Was this part of his religious regimen as a Jew? Yes. This discipline served as an anchor for him in a high-stress work environment. When faced with situations that could have cost him his life, Daniel found answers, fresh perspective, strategy, and strength for his professional journey on his knees.

Though you may not find it appropriate to kneel at work, you can always use your lunch break or step away for a five- or ten-minute break to close your eyes and pray.

## When Worlds Collide

The activity of prayer is humankind leveraging the legal right to invoke supernatural influence on earth. In essence, it is terrestrial authorization for celestial intervention.[12] It is a weapon and advantage that Daniel used when faced with challenging problems of his time. Despite all the knowledge Daniel had received from Babylon's training program, Philippians 4:6–7 suggests he had a discipline of tapping into something higher, a space his education and experience could not reach. The technology of prayer allowed Daniel to solve the complexities of his government that no one else on the king's council could. He had a spiritual discipline that distinguished him from some of the most competent men of the king's cabinet. The discipline of prayer kept

---

[12] Myles Munroe, *Understanding the Purpose and Power of Prayer* (New Kensington: Whitaker House, 2002).

Daniel grounded in his faith and emotionally balanced, and it granted him access to an open portal for revelatory insight. Through prayer, Daniel could see and forecast what others could not.

You were not meant to carry the weight of your job or business alone. In a climate where stress and anxiety run high, you can't afford not to pray! In prayer, solutions, peace, strength, joy, and soundness are realized. Access the supernatural through the technology of prayer!

# TEN

## Beyond the Read
### *Entrepreneurship*

Watch a video segment between Michael Kwame
and Richard Namme on entrepreneurship.
thebookten.com
Access code: DanielTEN

# TEN

## Beyond the Read
## *Women in the Marketplace*

Watch a video segment between Michael Kwame
and Tiffany Grant on women in the marketplace.
thebookten.com
Access code: DanielTEN

**CHAPTER 10**

# Ten Times Better

> The king talked with them, and out of them all not one was found like Daniel, Hananiah, Mishael and Azariah; so they entered the king's personal service. As for every matter of wisdom and understanding about which the king consulted them, he found them *ten times better* than all the magicians and conjurers who were in all his realm.
>
> —Daniel 1:19–21 (NASB; emphasis added)

Daniel worked for tyrants. It was the worst of circumstances. His employer could have staff members and advisers killed without a second thought. Daniel had to learn how to thrive during hostile Babylonian and Medo-Persian Empire takeovers. Through the chaos, the king found no one comparable to Daniel and his friends. Daniel 1:21 clearly states, "[The king] found them *ten times better*" (emphasis added). What was it about Daniel and his companions that made them ten times better than the rest? Let's start by looking at the significance of the number ten.

The number ten in Hebrew means "arm" or "hand." The arm or hand of God represents His power and intervention. It marks completion, order, and responsibility, as I said in the introduction to this book. God wants to move through you in your place of business. God wants to demonstrate His arm or hand through you to solve some of the most complex problems facing organizations today. He wants you to move in a spirit of excellence that is unmatched.

Daniel channeled the presence of God in a corrupt political climate, pairing his natural knowledge with revelation knowledge that he accessed through prayer and education.

There are a few things highlighted in this book and that are evident in the scriptures that I believe gave Daniel the competitive advantage:

- a strong relationship with God
- education and competence in his line of business (natural knowledge)
- integrity and character
- adaptability
- leadership capacity
- healthy lifestyle choices
- a network of professional colleagues and friends
- word of knowledge

You were born at a precise time for the complexities of this era. The ideas and solutions you carry are tailored for the challenges of this time. Every industry across the global landscape is crying out for a Daniel. Corporate, political, educational, social, ecclesiastical, technological, economic, and cultural climates are in need of effective leadership to inaugurate transformational paradigms. You are a solution bearer to an unsolved problem. Will you be a Daniel in your designated sphere of influence? May you rise above the status quo and be counted as *ten times better* in your generation!

# BIBLIOGRAPHY

Abbot, Lydia, Maria Ignatova, and Allison Schnidman. *30 Behavioral Interview Questions to Identify High-Potential Candidates*. LinkedIn Talent Solutions, 2017.

Bolz, Shawn. *God's Secrets: A Life Filled with Words of Knowledge*. Studio City: ICreate Productions, 2017.

Brooks, Leonard, and Paul Dunn. *Business and Professional Ethics*. Boston: Cengage Learning, 2015.

Connolly, Marie, and Margot Slade. "The United States of Stress 2019." Everyday Health. Last modified May 7, 2019. https://www.everydayhealth.com/wellness/united-states-of-stress.

Miller, S. M. *The Complete Guide to the Bible*. Phoenix: Barbour Publishing, 2007.

Munroe, Myles. *Understanding the Purpose and Power of Prayer*. New Kensington: Whitaker House, 2002.

Shotwell, Wesley. *The Power of Being a Servant*. Keller: Austin Brothers Publishing, 2011.

Swenson, Richard A. *Margin*. Colorado Springs: NavPress, 2004.

Printed in the United States
By Bookmasters